STATISTICS: SELECTED QUESTIONS AT HAND

SUPRIYA RAY

ISBN 979-888591531-1

Dedicated

to

Almighty

and

my parents

Late Satyapriya Ray and *Mrs.Bithika Ray*

Contents

Preface

This book is Written to cover the questions of undergraduate courses of all universities related to the Statistics. Also it can be a reference material for management Students, C.A and I.C.W.A Course and also for various Competitive examinations. The book has been written in a very simple style, to enable students to practice the subject effectively. What is more striking is that the answer of the mcq questions given behind every chapter would allure the students to solve them and enjoy their advancement. Regarding the organization the book is done well arranged in a coherent manner. I hope this book will satisfy all the requirements of the students for practicing the subject successfully and getting through the examination with flying colours.

I am thankful to Mr. Naveen Valsakum, chiref Executive officer, Mrs. Lekshmi Baskar, sr. Publishing consultant, and Mr. Yamini Shekar of Notion Press Publishing for accepting to publish the book.

I sincerely welcome criticism, views and suggestions from readers and conclude that this book would never have been written without the support, encouragement , and prodding of my family members. Many thanks all of them.

SUPRIYA RAY
supriyaray68@gmail.com

CHAPTER ONE

INTRODUCTION TO ORDINARDY VARIABLES

MCQ

Q.1 Which of the subsequent values is employed as a summary measure for a sample, like a sample mean?

(A) Population parameter

(B) Sample parameter

(C) Sample statistic

(D) Population mean

Answer: C

Q.2 Which of the subsequent could be a branch of statistics?

(A) Descriptive statistics

(B) Inferential statistics

(C) Industry statistics

(D) Both A and B

Answer: D

Q.3 The control charts and procedures of descriptive statistics which are accustomed enhance a procedure may be classified into which of those categories?

(A) Behavioural tools

(B) Serial tools

(C) Industry statistics

(D) Statistical tools

Answer: D

Q.4 Which of the subsequent may also be represented as sample statistics?

(A) Lowercase Greek letters

(B) roman print

(C) Associated Roman alphabets

(D) Uppercase Greek letters

Answer: B

Q.5 To which of the subsequent options do individual respondents, focus groups, and panels of respondents belong?

A) Primary data sources

B) Secondary data sources

C) Itemised data sources

D) Pointed data sources

Answer: A

Q.6 What are the variables whose calculation is finished in line with the load, height, and length known as?

(A) Flowchart variables

(B) Discrete variables

(C) Continuous variables

(D) Measuring variables

Answer: C

Q.7 Which method accustomed examine rate of inflation anticipation, per centum, and capacity utilisation to supply products?

(A) Data exporting technique

(B) Data importing technique

(C) Forecasting technique

(D) Data supplying technique

Answer: C

Q.8 Specialised processes like graphical and numerical methods are utilised during which of the following?

(A) Education statistics

(B) Descriptive statistics

(C) Business statistics

(D) Social statistics

Answer: B

Q.9 what's the size applied in statistics, which imparts a difference of magnitude and proportions, is taken into account as?

(A) Exponential scale

(B) Goodness scale

(C) Ratio scale

(D) Satisfactory scale

Answer: C

Q.10 Review of performance appraisal, labour turnover rates, planning of incentives, and training programs are the samples of which of the following?

(A) Statistics in production

(B) Statistics in marketing

(C) Statistics in finance

(D) Statistics in personnel management

Answer: D

SAQ

1) What do you mean by statistics? Define its various types with the help of examples of daily life.

2) "Statistical methods are most dangerous tools in the hand of inexpert." Discuss briefly

3) Define following concepts: i) Descriptive statistics ii) Inferential statistics iii) Parametric statistics iv) Non parametric statistics

4) Comments on the following statements in two or three lines with reasons: i) Statistics in singular sense implies statistical methods. ii) Statistics and statistic implies same thing. iii) Statistics may rightly be called the science of averages. iv) There are lies, damn lies and statistics. Give three examples of misuse of statistics.

5) Write a note on the limitations of statistics.

6) What do you mean by Descriptive statistics? Discuss its importance briefly.

7) Define the following terms: i) Class interval ii) Upper limit of class interval iii) lower limit of class interval, iv) Midpoint of class interval

8) What do you mean by organisation of data ? Describe various methods for organising data.

9) How can you describe the data? State the various types of measures of central tendency and their respective uses.

10) What do you mean by measures of dispersion? Explain why the range is relatively unstable measures of variability

11) Explain the importance of inferential statistics.

12) Describe the important properties of good estimators.

13) What do you mean by statement of hypothesis?

14) Discuss the different types of hypothesis formulated in hypothesis testing .

15) Discuss the errors involved in hypothesis testing.

16) Explain the concept of level of significance, one tail test, two tail test and power of a test.

17) Explain the various steps involved in hypothesis testing.

CHAPTER TWO

CLASSIFICATION & TABULATION

MCQ

Question 1 What is the arrangement of data in rows and columns known as?

(A) Frequency distribution
(B) Cumulative frequency distribution
(C) Tabulation
(D) Classification
Answer: C

Question 2When the quantitative and qualitative data are arranged according to a single feature, what is the tabulation known as?

(A) One-way
(B) Bivariate
(C) Manifold division
(D) Dichotomy
Answer: A

Question 3Which function does the tabulation origin spot specify?

(A) The list of integers
(B) The list of maxterms
(C) The list of minterms
(D) None of the above
Answer: A

Question 4 What does the tabulation form exercise?

(A) Gates
(B) Demorgan's postulate

(C) Matching process cycle

(D) Venn diagram

Answer: C

Question 5What was the first tabulation method known as?

(A) Quine-McCluskey

(B) Cluskey

(C) McQuine

(D) None of the above

Answer: D

Question 6What is the table where the variables are subdivided with interrelated features known as?

(A) Order level table

(B) Sub-parts of a table

(C) One-way table

(D) Two-way table

Answer: D

Question7In a tabular presentation, what is the summary and presentation of data with different non-overlapping classes defined as?

(A) Frequency distribution

(B) Chronological distribution

(C) Ordinal distribution

(D) Nominal distribution

Answer: A

Question 8 What are the general tables of data used to show data in an orderly manner known as?

(A) Double characteristic tables

(B) Manifold tables

(C) Repository tables

(D) Single characteristics tables

Answer: C

Question 9- Which of the following is the objective of classification?

a. To condense the mass of data.

b. To present data in a simple, logical, and understandable form.

c. To bring out points of similarity and dissimilarity among various groups.

d. All of the above

Answer: d

Question 10-Temperature, height, weight, marks are an example of ________.

a. Discrete variables
b. Continuous variables
c. Both a. and b.
d. None of the above
Answer: b

SAQ

1) What do you mean by classification? Discuss its various methods with suitable examples.

2) Following are the marks obtained by 30 students of psychology in their annual examination. Classify them in a frequency table. 30, 35, 36, 35, 19, 25, 63, 50, 32, 58, 55, 28, 43, 19, 40, 51, 56, 15, 14, 31, 56, 62, 22, 46, 52, 17, 54, 37, 16, 50

3) State different parts of of a statistical table.

4) Distinguish between classification and tabulation

5) Differentiate between the following pairs of terms i) Histogram and bar diagram ii) Frequency polygon and cumulative frequency curve iii) Sub-divided bar diagram and multiple bar diagram.

6) Explain the following terms: i) Frequency polygon ii) Bar diagram iii) Subdivided bar diagram iv) Multiple bar diagram v) Pie diagram

7) Differentiate between following pairs of statistical terms i) Column and row entry ii) Caption and stub head iii) Head note and foot note

8) What points are to be kept in mind while taking decision for preparing a frequency distribution in respect of (a) the number of classes and (b) width of class interval

9) State briefly the importance of tabulation in statistical analysis.

10)Describe: Cumulative Frequency Curve or Ogive

CHAPTER THREE

DIAGRAMMATIC REPRESENTATION OF DATA

MCQ

1. Histogram represents ________ series.

(a.) Individual series

(b.) Discrete series

(c.) Continuous series

(d.) None of the above

Answers: c

2.Frequency polygon is obtained by joining _________.

(a.) Mid points of tops of rectangles

(b.) Two end points

(c.) End Points of first class interval

(d.) End points of last class interval

Answers: a

3.Ogive represents __________ on a graph.

(a.) Individual frequencies

(b.) Cumula tive frequencies

(c.) Frequency polygon

(d.) Frequency curve

Answers: b

4.Less than ogive can be used to calculate __________.

(a.) Range

(b.) Arithmetic mean

(c.) Mode

(d.) Median

Answers: d

5. What is taken on X-axis while using time series graphs?

(a.) Income

(b.)Exports

(c.)Imports

(d.) Time

Answers: (d)

SAQ

1. What is diagrammatic presentation of data?
2. Explain the importance and limitations of diagrammatic presentation of data.
3. What is graphical presentation of data?
4. Explain the importance and limitations of graphical presentation of data.
5. What is false base line? When is it used?
6. Distinguish: Diagrammatic and Graphical presentation of data
7. Distinguish: Bar Diagram and Histogram
8. Distinguish: Histogram and Historigram
9. Distinguish: Mixed Graph and Range Graph
10. Distinguish: One dimensional diagram and two dimensional diagrams
11. How is Histrogram constructed when class intervals are of unequal width?
12. Short note on histogram
13. Short note on historigram
14. Short note on ogive
15. Short note on frequency curve
16. Short note on frequency polygon
17. Short note on false base line
18. Distinguish: Less than Ogive and More than Ogive
19. Distinguish: Bar Diagram and Pie Diagram
20. Distinguish: Frequency Curve and Frequency Polygon.

CHAPTER FOUR

MEASURES OF CENTRAL TENDENCY

MCQ

1. The range of a sample gives an indication of the

(A) way in which the values cluster about a particular point

(B) number of observations bearing the same value

(C) maximum variation in the sample

(D) degree to which the mean value differs from its expected value.

Answers: (c)

2. The observation which occurs most frequently in a sample is the

(A) median

(B) mean deviation

(C) standard deviation

(D) mode

Answers: (d)

3. What is the median of the sample 5, 5, 11, 9, 8, 5, 8 ?

(A) 5

(B) 6

(C) 8

(D) 9

Answers: (c)

5. The value obtained by reciprocating the mean of the reciprocal of x1, x2, x3, ... Xn observations is called

(A) Arithmetic mean

(B) harmonic mean

(C) standard mean

(D) geometric mean

Answers: (B)

6. When numbers are associated with weights, then the obtained mean is said to be

(A) weighted arithmetic mean

(B) harmonic mean

(C) standard mean

(D) geometric mean

Answers: (A)

7. The arithmetic mean of the values 2, 7, 9, 18 is equal to

(A) 7

(B) 8

(C) 9

(D) 11

Answers: (B)

8. The median, mode, deciles and percentiles are all considered as measures of

(a) mathematical averages

(b) population averages

(c) sample averages

(d)averages of position

Answers: (d)

9. The total of all the observations divided by the number of observations is called:

(a) Arithmetic mean

(b) Geometric mean

(c) Median

(d) Harmonic mean

Answers: (A)

10. The arithmetic mean is highly affected by:

(a) Moderate values

(b) Extremely small values

(c) Odd values

(d) Extremely large values

Answers: (d)

11. The elimination of extreme scores at the bottom of the set has the effect of:

(a) Lowering the mean

(b) Raising the mean

(c) No effect

(d) None of the above

Answers: (b)

12. The mean of 10 observations is 10. All the observations are increased by 10%. The mean of increased observations will be:

(a) 10

(b) 1.1

(c) 10.1

(d) 11

Answers: (d)

13.We must arrange the data before calculating:

(a) Mean

(b) Median

(c) Mode

(d) Geometric mean

Answers: (b)

14. If the smallest observation in a data is decreased, the average which is not affected is:

(a) Mode

(b) Median

(c) Mean

(d) Harmonic mean

Answers: (b)

15. Sum of absolute deviations of the values is least when deviations are taken from:

(a) Mean

(b) Mode

(c) Median

(d) Q3

Answers: (C)

SAQ

1. Define average. State the objectives and essentials of an ideal average.

2. State the meaning, properties, merits and limitations of arithmetic mean.

3. (a) State the meaning, properties, merits and limitations of arithmetic median.

(b) Why the median called a positional average?

4. State the meaning, properties, merits and limitations of mode.

5. State the meaning, properties, merits and limitations of geometric mean.

6. State the meaning, properties, merits and limitations of harmonic mean

7. State two practical situations where you will recommend the use of (a) Median (b) Mode (c) Geometric Mean and (d) Harmonic Mean.

8. Under what circumstances would it be appropriate to use Median or Mode, Harmonic Mean or Geometric Mean?

9. Prove that the sum of deviations of observations from their arithmetic mean is zero.

10. Compare and contrast arithmetic mean, geometric mean and harmonic mean. Which of them is least affected by extreme values?

11. Define Weighted Arithmetic Mean, Weighted Geometric Mean and Weighted Harmonic Mean. Under what circumstances would you recommend their use?

12. How do you make a choice of suitable measure of Central Tendency!

13. List the cases in which Arithmetic Mean should not be used.

14. Give a specific example of your own for each of the following cases:

(i) The median is preferred to the arithmetic mean.

(ii) The harmonmic mean is preferred to the arithmetic mean.

(iii) The mode will be preferred to the median.

(iv) The arithmetic mean is preferred to the harmonic mean.

(v) No average would be meaningful.

15. Suggest suitable averages for the following cases:

(i) The sizes of garments sold out in a garment shop.

(ii) The distribution with open-ended classes.

(iii) Average rate of growth required from the figures of percentage changes from year (iv) The distance is fixed but the speeds are varying.

(v) When it is desired that the absolute sum of the deviations from that average is minimum.

(vi) When it is desired to iron out irregular fluctuations in the time-series data.

(vii) If the purpose is to give small items more importance than the big items.

(viii) If the distribution has extreme items.

(ix) The cost of living index is to be constructed.

(x) In making the preference of furniture style from the available styles.

(xi) If the purpose is to give a little more importance than big item. [(i) Mode (ii) Median (iii) G.M. (iv) H.M. (v) Median (vi) Moving Average (vii) H.M. (viii) Median (ix) Weighted Average (x) Mode (xi) G.M.]

16. The average salary paid to all workers of a company is Rs. 500. Average salaries paid to skilled and unskilled workers are Rs. 520 and Rs. 420 respectively. Determine the percentage of skilled and unskilled workers.

17. Arithmetic mean of 100 items was found to be 50.8. It was later discovered, one item 47 was wrongly taken as 67. Find the correct mean.

18. Arithmetic mean of 50 items was found as 28.5. It was latcr found that item 39 was taken extra. Find the correct mean of 49 items

19. Prices of three commodities viz... A, B & C rised by 40 %, 60% and 90% respectively. Commodity A is six times more important than C, and B is three times more important than C. What is the mean rise in price of these three commodities?

20. The annual growth rate of production of a factory in 5 years is 5.0, 7.5, 5.0, 2.5 and 10 per cent. respectively. What is the compound rate of growth of production per annum for the period.

CHAPTER FIVE

MEASURES OF DISPERSION

MCQ

1. The scatter in a series of values about the average is called:

(a) Central tendency

(b) Dispersion

(c) Skewness

(d) Symmetry

Answers: (b)

2. The measurements of spread or scatter of the individual values around the central point is called:

(a) Measures of dispersion

(b) Measures of central tendency

(c) Measures of skewness

(d) Measures of kurtosis

Answers: (A)

3. The measures used to calculate the variation present among the observations relative to their average is called:

(a) Coefficient of kurtosis

(b) Absolute measures of dispersion

(c) Quartile deviation

(d) Relative measures of dispersion

Answers: (D)

4. The degree to which numerical data tend to spread about an average value called:

(a) Constant

(b) Flatness

(c) Variation

(d) Skewness

Answers: (C)

5. Given below the four sets of observations. Which set has the minimum variation?

(a) 46, 48, 50, 52, 54

(b) 30, 40, 50, 60, 70

(c) 40, 50, 60, 70, 80

(d) 48, 49, 50, 51, 52

Answers: (D)

6. Half of the difference between upper and lower quartiles is called:

(a) Interquartile range

(b) Quartile deviation

(c) Mean deviation

(d) Standard deviation

Answers: (B)

7. Which measure of dispersion can be computed in case of open-end classes?

(a) Standard deviation

(b) Range

(c) Quartile deviation

(d) Coefficient of variation

Answers: (C)

8. S.D(X) = 6 and S.D(Y) = 8. If X and Yare independent random variables, then S.D(X-Y) is:

(a) 2

(b) 10

(c) 14

(d) 100

Answers: (B)

9. Which of the following statements is correct?

(a) The standard deviation of a constant is equal to unity

(b) The sum of absolute deviations is minimum if these deviations are taken from the mean.

(c) The second moment about origin equals variance

(d) The variance is positive quantity and is expressed in square of the units of the observations

Answers: (D)

10. Which of the following statements is false?

(a) The standard deviation is independent of change of origin

(b) If the moment coefficient of kurtosis $\beta 2 = 3$, the distribution is mesokurtic or normal.

(c) If the frequency curve has the same shape on both sides of the centre line which divides the curve into two equal parts, is called a symmetrical distribution.

(d) Variance of the sum or difference of any two variables is equal to the sum of their respective variances

Answers: (D)

11. The first moment about X = 0 of a distribution is 12.08. The mean is:

(a) 10.80

(b) 10.08

(c) 12.08

(d) 12.88

Answers: (C)

12. First two moments about the value 2 of a variable are 1 and 16. The variance will be:

(a) 13

(b) 15

(c) 16

(d) Difficult to tell

Answers: (B)

13. If the third central is negative, the distribution will be:

(a) Symmetrical

(b) Positively skewed

(c) Negatively skewed

(d) Normal

Answers: (C)

14. If the third moment about mean is zero, then the distribution is:

(a) Positively skewed

(b) Negatively skewed

(c) Symmetrical

(d) Mesokurtic

Answers: (C)

15. If mean=10, median=8 and standard deviation=6, then coefficient of skewness is:

(a) 1

(b) -1
(c) 2/6
(d) 2
Answers: (A)

SAQ

1. Define Dispersion.
2. Define Range.
3. Define Quartile Deviation.
4. Define Mean Deviation.
5. Define Standard Deviation.
6. Define Coefficient of Variation.
7. Define Variance.
8. Define Lorenz Curve.
9. Name the measure of variation that is least affected by extreme observations.
10. Name the measure of variation which is least when deviations are taken from arithmetic mean
11. State the methods of measuring dispersion.
12. State the merits of Range.
13. State the limitations of Range.
14. State the merits of Quartile Deviation.
15. State the limitations of Quartile Deviation.
16. State the merits of Mean Deviation.
17. State the limitations of Mean Deviation.
18. State the properties of Standard Deviation.
19. State the merits of Standard Deviation. 20. State the limitations of Standard Deviation.
21. State the object of Coefficient of Variation.
22. State the uses of Dispersion. N
23. State the characteristics of a good measure of dispersion.
24. State the steps involved in drawing Lorenz Curve.
25. Distinguish between absolute and relative measures of dispersion.
26. Why is standard deviation considered to be the most reliable measure of dispersion?
27. Find Standard Deviation of a natural numbers.

28. Name the measure of variation which is least when deviations are taken from median

29. Name the measure of central tendency which is used in Standard Deviation.

30. State the relationship between Quartile Deviation and Standard Deviation.

CHAPTER SIX

METHODS OF MOMENTS

MCQ

1. The first three moments of a distribution about the mean X are 1, 4 and 0. The distribution is:

a. Symmetrical
b. Skewed to the left
c. Skewed to the right
d. Normal
answer: (A)

2. For a positively skewed distribution, mean is always:

a. Less than the median
b. Less than the mode
c. Greater than the mode
d. Difficult to tell
answer: (C)

3. Bowley's coefficient of skewness lies between:

a. 0 and 1
b. 1 and +1
c. -1 and 0
d. -2 and +2
answer: (B)

4. The second and fourth moments about mean are 4 and 48 respectively, then the distribution is:

a. Leptokurtic
b. Platykurtic
c. Mesokurtic or normal
d. Positively skewed

answer: (C)

5. The measures used to calculate the variation present among the observations in the unit of the variable is called:

a. Relative measures of dispersion

b. Coefficient of skewness

c. Absolute measures of dispersion

d. Coefficient of variation

answer: (C)

6. The measure of dispersion which uses only two observations is called:

a. Mean

b. Median

c. Range

d. Coefficient of variation

answer: (c)

7. Half of the difference between upper and lower quartiles is called:

a. Interquartile range

b. Quartile deviation

c. Mean deviation

d. Standard deviation

answer: (B)

8. The mean deviation of the scores 12, 15, 18 is:

a. 6

b. 0

c. 3

d. 2

answer: (D)

9. The variance is zero only if all observations are the:

a. Different

b. Square

c. Square root

d. Same

answer: (D)

10. The standard deviation of -5, -5, -5, -5, 5 is:

a. -5

b. +5

c. 0

d. -25

answer: (C)

SAQ

1. What is skewness?
2. State the shape of unimodel symmetrical distribution.
3. State the shape of bimodel symmetrical distribution.
4. Name the distribution in which frequencies are highest in the higher values.
5. Name the distribution in which frequencies are highest in the lower values.
6. Name the distribution in which frequencies are highest in the lower values.
7. Name the distribution in which frequencies are lowest in the lower values,
8. Name the distribution in which the sum of positive and negative deviations from median is always equal to zero
9. State the relationship between mean, median and mode in case of a unimodel symmetrical distribution.
10. State the relationship between mean, median and mode in case of a bimodel symmetrical distribution.
11. State the relationship between means median and mode in case of a positively skewed distribution.
12. State the relationship between mean, median and mode in case of a negatively skewed distribution.
13. State the main characteristics of a positively skewed distribution.
14. State the main characteristics of a negatively skewed distribution.
15. State the main characteristics of a J-shaped positively skewed distribution. Thy To Dr
16. State the main characteristics of a J-shaped negatively skewed distribution.
17. State the main characteristics of a U-shaped Bimodel symmetrical distribution.
18. State the formula for measuring absolute skewness when mode is defined.
19. State the formula for measuring absolute skewness when mode is ill-defined.

20. State the formula for measuring absolute skewness on the basis of quartiles.

21. State the relationship between the following in case of skewed distribution,

(i) a positively skewed distribution, (ii) a negatively, (iii) symmetrical distribution.

(a) Mean and Mode

(b) Mean and Median

(c) Quartiles

22. State the formula for measuring Karl Pearson's Coefficient of skewness if mode is defined.

23. State the formula for measuring Karl Pearson's coefficient of skewness if mode is ill-defined.

24. State the range of Karl Pearons's coefficient of skewness.

25. State the formula for quartile measure of skewness. State the form

26. State the range of quartile measure of skewness.

27. the formula for percentile measure of skewness. State the

28. State the formula for decile measure of skewness.

29. State whether the coefficient of skewness will be (a) Zero (B) Positive or (c) Negative in each of the following distribution.

(i) Bell-shaped

(ii) U-shaped

(iii) J-shaped

(iv) L-shaped

30. Calculate karl pearson's coefficient of skewness if mean 65, mode 80, variance 625.

31. Why are the measures of skewness calculated?

32. Distinguish between skewness and disperson.

33. List the tests that are applied to find out presence or absence of skewness in distribution.

34. State the empirical relationship among mean, median and mode in a symmetrical and a moderately asymmetrical distribution. How does it help in estimating mode and measuring skewness?

35. State two uses quartile measure of skewness.

36. Define Moments and State their usefulness in statistical analysis.

37. Show the relationship between the central moments and raw-moments.

38. State Sheppard's corrections and their conditions for their applicability.

39. (a) Define Kurtosis and State the measures of kurtosis. (b) Distinguish between skewness and kurtosis.

40. Calculate karl pearson's coefficient of skewness if mean 20, median 17, variance 16.

CHAPTER SEVEN

BIVARIATE DATA ANALYSIS

MCQ

1. Which of the following cannot be covered under univariate analysis of data?

a. Association between two variables
b. Computation of mean, median and mode
c. Preparation of frequency table
d. Computation of percentage frequency for a variable
Answers: (A)

2. Both mean and mode can be computed for what type of measurement scales.

a. Nominal
b. Ordinal
c. Interval
d. Ratio
e. c and d
f. a and c
Answers: (E)

3. Which of the following option is not available for the treatment of missing value?

a. Substitute the average value of the response
b. Substitute a neutral value
c. Return to the field to get the desired observation
d. The concerned questionnaire should be eliminated from the analysis.
Answers: (C)

4. In the interpretation of the cross table, the percentages should be computed

a. Row wise

b. Column wise

c. In the direction of the independent variable

d. Computing percentages either row wise or column wise does not make a difference.

Answers: (C)

5. For which type of measurement, the coefficient of variation can be computed.

a. Nominal scale

b. Ordinal scale

c. Interval scale

d. Ratio scale

Answers: (D)

6. A third variable is introduced in the two variable table to

a. Refine the association that was observed originally between two variables.

b. The introduction of third variable may show that there was no association between the original two variables.

c. Introducing a third variable may indicate association between two original variables although initially no relationship was found between them.

d. All of the above are true.

Answers: (D)

7. Which of the following is true about the missing observation?

a. Missing value could be coded with another number which should not be equal to the value of the variable obtained as a part of the survey.

b. It is possible to get different research conclusions if the value of the missing observation was available.

c. The actual results may deviate from the observed results depends upon the number of missing observation and the extent to which the missing data would be different from the actual observation.

d. All of the above statements are true.

Answers: (D)

8. Which of the following is true in case of interpretation of a table with analysis of multiple responses?

a. The percentages add up to 100%.

b. The percentages exceed 100% because of multiplicity of answer.

c. The percentages cannot be computed.

d. All the above statements are incorrect.

Answers: (B)

9. There are 20% female students in a class – this is an example of

a. Descriptive analysis

b. Inferential analysis

c. Gender bias

d. All of the above are correct

Answers: (A)

10. For which type of measurement, median cannot be computed.

a. Nominal

b. Ordinal

c. Interval

d. Ratio

Answers: (A)

11. Which of the following analysis cannot be carried out using ordinal scale data?

a. Preparation of frequency distribution

b. Computation of the quartiles of the distribution

c. Computing the mode of the distribution

d. Computing the standard deviation of the variable

Answers: (D)

12. The uses of a frequency distribution are

a. To get the extent of non response.

b. To detect the presence of extreme cases (outliers in the distribution).

c. To get the extent of illegitimate responses.

d. All of the above

Answers: (D)

13. That measure of central tendency above which 50% values fall and below which the remaining 50% fall is called:

a. Mean

b. Median

c. Mode

d. Range

Answers: (B)

14. When a respondent assigns an order of preference using values as 1, 2, 3 and so on, he is using

a. Nominal values

b. Ordinal values

c. Interval values

d. Ratio values

Answers: (B)

15. The median can be computed from

a. Ordinal, interval and nominal data

b. Ratio, ordinal and nominal data

c. Ratio, interval and ordinal data

d. Ratio, interval and nominal data

Answers: (C)

16. Which of the following gives the measure of consistency of data?

a. Mean

b. Standard deviation

c. Mode

d. Median

Answers: (B)

17. The simple way to look at association for the data which requires only the ability to compute percentages.

a. Cross-tabulation

b. Correlation coefficient

c. Spearman rank correlation coefficient

d. Simple graph

e. None of the above

Answers: (A)

18. Factor analysis is a technique for

a. Univariate data

b. Bivariate data

c. Multivariate data

d. Both (a) and (b)

e. Both (a) and (c)

f. Both (b) and (c)

Answers: (C)

19. Which of the following may not be the right method for dealing with missing information on a questionnaire?

a. Discard the questionnaire

b. Ignore that particular question and code the remaining

c. Based on responses of similar respondents, substitute a value

d. All of them may be appropriate

e. Both (a) and (b)

f. Both (b) and (c)

Answers: (D)

20. Median can be computed for

a. Closed ended class interval

b. Open ended class interval

c. Ordinal scale data

d. Interval scale data

e. Ratio scale data

f. All of them are true

Answers: (F)

SAQ

A. CORRELATION

1. (a) What is correlation? State three instances each of its use in the field of economics and commerce.

(b) Does it always signify cause and effect relationship between two variables?

(c) How is the coefficient of correlation interpreted?

(d) Enumerate the various methods available for finding the correlation.

2. (a) What is scatter diagram?

(b) Indicate by means of suitable scatter diagrams different types of correlation that may exist between the variables in a bivariate data.

(c) How is it useful in the study of correlation?

3. (a) Define Karl Pearson's coefficient of correlation.

(b) State the properties of Pearson's coefficient of correlation.

(c) How would you interpret the value of r?

(d) Why is it termed as the coefficient of linear correlation? Explain.

4. (a) Explain the term probable error of r?

(b) State the significance of probable error of r.

5. (a) Define rank correlation.

(b) Write down Spearman's formula for rank correlation coefficient.

(c) What are the limits of r,?

(d) Interpret the case when r, assumed the minimum value.

(e) State the merits and demerits of Spearman's rank correlation.

(f) When is it preferred to Karl Pearson's coefficient of correlation?

6. (a) Prove that the correlation coefficient is independent of change of scale and origin.

(b) Prove that Karl Pearson's coefficient of correlation always lies between ± 1.

(c) Show that for two independent variants, correlation coefficient is zero.

7. Distinguish between the following:

(a) Positive, Negative and Zero Correlation

(b) Simple and Multiple Correlation

(c) Partial Multiple and Total Multiple Correlation

8. When can we say that two variables are correlated? What would you infer if Ery turns out to be zero?

9. The coefficient of rank correlation of a bivariate data is 1. Does it imply perfect correlation between the variables? Give reasons for your answer.

10. If the product moment coefficient of correlation is 0. does it mean that the variances are independent? Is the converse true?

B. REGRESSION

1. What is meant by regression?
2. What is meant by regression analysis?
3. What is meant by regression equation?
4. What is meant by regression line?
5. What is meant by regression coefficients?
6. Can there be one regression line? If yes, specify the situation.
7. State why there are in general two lines of regression.
8. When do regression lines coincide?
9. Write down the equation of Y on X.
10. Write down the equation of X on Y
11. Write the two normal equations for regression equation of Y on X.
12. Write the two normal equations for regression equation of X on Y.
13. State the relations between coefficient of correlation and regression.
14. What is regression? What is its significance in economic analysis?
15. (a) What are regression lines?

(b) Why are there in general two regression lines?

(c) When do they coincide?

(d) Can there be one regression line? If yes, specify the situation.

(e) Write two normal equations for regression lines.

CHAPTER EIGHT

INDEX NUMBER

MCQ

1. An index number is called a simple index when it is computed from:

(a) Single variable

(b) Bi-variable

(c) Multiple variables

(d) None of them

Answers: (A)

2.Index numbers are expressed in:

(a) Ratios

(b) Squares

(c) Percentages

(d) Combinations

Answers: (C)

3. If all the values are of equal importance, the index numbers are called:

(a) Weighted

(b) Unweighted

(c) Composite

(d) Value index

Answers: (B)

4. Index numbers can be used for:

(a) Forecasting

(b) Fixed prices

(c) Different prices

(d) Constant prices

Answers: (A)

5. Index for base period is always taken as:

(a) 100

(b) One

(c) 200

(d) Zero

Answers: (A)

6. When the prices of rice are to be compared, we compute:

(a) Volume index

(b) Value index

(c) Price index

(d) Aggregative index

Answers: (C)

7. When index number is calculated for several variables, it is called:

(a) Composite index

(b) Whole sale price index

(c) Volume index

(d) Simple index

Answers: (A)

8. How many types are used for the calculation of index numbers:

(a) 2

(b) 3

(c) 4

(d) 5

Answers: (A)

9. In chain base method, the base period is:

(a) Fixed

(b) Not fixed

(c) Constant

(d) Zero

Answers: (B)

10.An index number that can serve many purposes is called:

(a) General purpose index

(b) Special purpose index

(c) Cost of living index

(d) None of them

Answers: (A)

11. Consumer price index numbers are obtained by:

(a) Laspeyre's formula

(b) Fisher ideal formula

(c) Marshall Edgeworth formula

(d) Paasche's formula

Answers: (A)

12. Most commonly used index number is:

(a) Volume index number

(b) Value index number

(c) Price index number

(d) Simple index number

Answers: (C)

13. Consumer price index are obtained by:

(a) Paasche's formula

(b) Fisher's ideal formula

(c) Marshall Edgeworth formula

(d) Family budget method formula

Answers: (D)

14. The general purchasing power of the currency of a country is determined by:

(a) Retail price index

(b) Volume index

(c) Composite index

(d) Whole-sale price index

Answers: (D)

15. To measure the relative change in purchasing a specified basket of goods and services between two periods for a certain locality for fixed income group of people, we can use:

(a) Consumer price index

(b) Paasche's price index

(c) Cost of living index

(d) Both (a) and (c)

Answers: (D)

SAQ

1) A composite price index where the prices of the items in the composite are weighted by their relative importance is known as ?

2) A weighted aggregate price index where the weight for each item is its current-period quantity is called ?

3) An index that is designed to measure changes in quantities over time is known as ?

4) If the wholesale price index for week 1is 200 and for week 2 is 250 then rate of inflation is?

5.What is value relative?

6.State the characteristics of index number.

7.Mention the uses of index number.

8.Mention the steps used in the construction of index number

9.Name the index number that satisfies TRT.

10.Name the index number that satisfies that FRT.

11.What is consumer price index number?

12. What are the uses of CPI?

13. Explain briefly the steps in the construction of consumer price index number.

14. Define weighted index number.

15. Define consumer price index number.

16. What is the wholesale price index?

17. What should be the base year like?

18. Name the consumer groups for which the consumer price index number is computed.

19. Name one principal limitation of index numbers.

20. Explain price relative.

21. Why do we need an index number?

22. What are the desirable properties of the base period?

23. Why is it essential to have different CPI for different categories of consumers?

24. What does a consumer price index for industrial workers measure?

25. What is the difference between a price index and a quantity index?

26. Is the change in any price reflected in a price index number?

27. Can the CPI for urban non-manual employees represent the changes in the cost of living of the President of India?

28. If the salary of a person in the base year is Rs 4,000 per annum and the current year salary is Rs 6,000, by how much should his salary be raised to maintain the same standard of living if the CPI is 400?

29. The consumer price index for June, 2005 was 125. The food index was 120 and that of other items 135. What is the percentage of the total weight given to food?

30. Why fishers index number is the ideal index number?

CHAPTER NINE

TIME SERIES ANALYSIS

MCQ

1. An orderly set of data arranged in accordance with their time of occurrence is called:

(a) Arithmetic series
(b) Harmonic series
(c) Geometric series
(d) Time series
Answers: (D)

2. A time series consists of:

(a) Short-term variations
(b) Long-term variations
(c) Irregular variations
(d) All of the above
Answers: (D)

3. The graph of time series is called:

(a) Histogram
(b) Straight line
(c) Historigram
(d) Ogive
Answers: (C)

4. Secular trend can be measured by:

(a) Two methods
(b) Three methods
(c) Four methods
(d) Five methods
Answers: (C)

5. The secular trend is measured by the method of semi-averages when:

(a) Time series based on yearly values

(b) Trend is linear

(c) Time series consists of even number of values

(d) None of them

Answers: (B)

6. Increase in the number of patients in the hospital due to heat stroke is:

(a) Secular trend

(b) Irregular variation

(c) Seasonal variation

(d) Cyclical variation

Answers: (C)

7. The systematic components of time series which follow regular pattern of variations are called:

(a) Signal

(b) Noise

(c) Additive model

(d) Multiplicative model

Answers: (A)

8. The unsystematic sequence which follows irregular pattern of variations is called:

(a) Noise

(b) Signal

(c) Linear

(d) Non-linear

Answers: (A)

9. In time series seasonal variations can occur within a period of:

(a) Four years

(b) Three years

(c) One year

(d) Nine years

Answers: (C)

10. Wheat crops badly damaged on account of rains is:

(a) Cyclical movement

(b) Random movement

(c) Secular trend

(d) Seasonal movement

Answers: (B)

11. The method of moving average is used to find the:

(a) Secular trend

(b) Seasonal variation

(c) Cyclical variation

(d) Irregular variation

Answers: (A)

12. A complete cycle consists of a period of:

(a) Prosperity and depression

(b) Prosperity and recovery

(c) Prosperity and recession

(d) Recession and recovery

Answers: (C)

13. A complete cycle passes through:

(a) Two stages

(b) Three stages

(c) Four stages

(d) Difficult to tell

Answers: (C)

14. Indicate which of the following an example of seasonal variations is:

(a) Death rate decreased due to advance in science

(b) The sale of air condition increases during summer

(c) Recovery in business

(d) Sudden causes by wars

Answers: (B)

15. In moving average method, we cannot find the trend values of some:

(a) Middle periods

(b) End periods

(c) Starting periods

(d) Between extreme periods

Answers: (D)

SAQ

1. Define Time Series.

2. Define Secular Trend.
3. Define Short-term Oscillations.
4. Define Seasonal Variations.
5. Define Cyclical Variations.
6. Define Irregular or Random Variations.
7. Define Dereasonalizing.
8. Define Moving Averages.
9. Write down straight line trend equation.
10. Write down quadratic trend equation.
11. Write down exponential trend equation.
12. What are the commonly used models in a time series analysis?
13. Express Additive Model.
14. Express Multiplicative Model.
15. In the trend equation Y = a + bX, what do ‘a’ and ‘b’ denote?
16. Enumerate the uses of analysis of time series.
17. What are the components of time series?
18. Distinguish between the following:

(a) Additive Model and Multiplicative Model of time series.

(b) Secular Trend and Seasonal Variation in time series.

(c) Ratio to Trend and Ratio to Moving Average Method.

(d) Seasonal Variations and Cyclical Variations.

19. "All period variations are not necessarily seasonal". Discuss this statement with suitable example
20. Write down normal equations for straight line trend equation.

CHAPTER TEN

VITAL STATISTICS

MCQ

1. What is the definition of sex ratio?

(a) Number of deaths per 1,000 live births of children

(b) Number of women per 1000 men

(c) Number of women per 100000 men

(d) Number of men per 1000 women

Answer: b

2. What does infant mortality mean?

(a) The number of deaths per 1,000 live births of children under 1 year of age

(b) Death of children under the age of 5 years

(c) Death of children before the age of 6 months

(d) Death of children under the age of 3 years

Answer: a

3. Which age group is included to calculate Child Sex Ratio?

(a) 1-6 years

(b) 0-5 years

(c) 0-6 years

(d) 0- 6 months

Answer: c

4. Which statement is NOT correct in respect to Child Sex Ratio?

(a) Arunachal Pradesh has the highest sex ratio in all states of India

(b) Kerala has the highest sex ratio in all states of India

(c) Haryana has the lowest sex ratio in all states of India

(d) Child sex ratio has decreased in 2011 as compared to 2001 census

Answer: b

5. What is the Maternal Mortality Rate?

(a) Women's death occurred before 9th month of pregnancy

(b) The annual number of female deaths per 100,000 live births due to pregnancy.

(c) The death of women occurred within 2 year of childbirth

(d) None of the above

Answer: b

6. What is the correct descending order on the basis of the number of sex ratio in the states?

(a) Kerala <Chhattisgarh <Mizoram <Andhra Pradesh

(b) Arunachal Pradesh <Kerala <Manipur <Meghalaya

(c) Meghalaya <Kerala << Chhattisgarh <Tamilnadu

(d) Kerala <Tamil Nadu <Andhra Pradesh <Chhattisgarh

Answer: d

7. According to Census 2011, how much was the Total Fertility Rate (TFR) in India?

(a) 2.1

(b) 2.3

(c) 2.4

(d) 2.0

Answer: c

8. Which of the following statements is NOT true with reference to the Total Fertility Rate (TFR)?

(a) The number of children born in the entire reproduction period of a woman is called the Total Fertility Rate of that female

(b) Bihar has the highest "Total Fertility Rate" of 3.3 among Indian state

(c) The Total Fertility Rate (TFR) of West Bengal, Tamil Nadu and Delhi is equal

(d) In India Buddhism has the lowest "Total Fertility Rate".

Answer: d

9. According to the latest data released by the NITI Aayog in 2016; What is the Infant Mortality Rate in India in 2016?

(a) 42 per 1000 live births

(b) 34 per 1000 live births

(c) 29 per 1000 live births

(d) 54 per 1000 live births

Answer: b

10. Which states of India have the lowest and highest Infant Mortality Rate respectively?

(a) Kerala, Bihar
(b) Odisha, Jharkhand
(c) Goa, Madhya Pradesh
(d) Maharashtra, Uttar Pradesh
Answer: c

SAQ

1. Define rate and ratio as used in vital statistics.

2. Define crude death rate and age-specific death rate. What are the defects of crude death rate? How do you tell that age-specific death rate improves the crude death rate ?

3. Explain why crude death rate is not suitable for comparing the mortality situations of two countries. Discuss the use of standardised death rate in this connection.

4. Describe the structure of a life table. Explain how a life table may be constructed on the basis of age-specific death rates.

5. Define CBR, GFR, ASFR and TFR, indicating how each can be considered an improvement on the preceding measure.

6. Define GRR and NRR, and discuss how good they are as indices of population growth.

7. Read the following statements and state in each case what you understand by it;

(a) "The GFR of a country in a certain year is 95 per thousand."
(b) "The NRR for a country is 1.327",

8. Write a short note on mortality rates

9. Write a short note on comperative mortality index

10. Write a short note on life table and its uses.

11. Define rate and ratio of vital events and discuss their usefulness.

12. Define crude death rate and specific death rates, and discuss their merits and defects.

13. What is standardised death rate? Explain the difference between crude death rate and standardized death rate. Distinguish between direct and indirect standardization.

14. What is a life table ? Explain the different parts of a life table. How is it constructed?

Explain the different uses of life table.

15. Define crude birth rate and state its defects. Do you think that general fertility rate' and 'age specific fertility rates' are better than crude birth rate? Why?

16. Discuss how one can effect a comparison between the fertility situations prevailing in two different communities?

17. Explain the main columns of a complete life table, explaining their significance.

18. Why do we need standardised death rate? How is this rate constructed? Also describe the method of indirect standardization.

19. Define GRR and NRR and explain their uses for forecasting future population growth.

20. Explain why the CDR is generally unsuitable for comparing the mortality situations of two regions. Suggest a suitable method for making such a comparison. Distinguish, in this connection, between direct and indirect standardisation.

21. What is meant by crude rate of natural increase? What are its defects as a measure of population growth? In what way are the GRR and NRR better?

22. Explain why the CDR is generally unsuitable for comparing the mortality situations of two regions. Suggest a suitable method for making such a comparison. Distinguish, in this connection, between direct and indirect standardisation.

23. Explain the main columns of a complete life table, explaining their significance.

24. Merits and demerits of CDR

25. What is vital index

26) What are the important uses of vital statistics?

27) Briefly explain differtmt data sources for vital statistics.

28) The mid-year population and number of births occmed of a dibal community in Madhya Pradesh in 1995 are 40,000 and 1200 respectively. Find the crude birth rate.

29) The mid-year population and the number of deaths registered in 2001 for a town in Maharashtra among females are 25000 and 245 respectively. Find the crude death rate.

29) The annual natural increase, annual net migration, and annual mid-year population in 1998 for a region are recorded as 1500,500 and 50000 respectively. Find the rate of total increase.

30) According to mortality conditions in India for the year 2000, what mual premium would an Indian female have to pay on a whole life policy worth Ra. 100,000 if this life was assured at birth, assuming that the assurance office earns no income on its funds?

CHAPTER ELEVEN

METHOD OF INTERPOLATION

MCQ

1. Interpolation is done by
a) Curve fitting
b) Regression analysis
c) Curve fitting & Regression analysis
d) None of the mentioned

Answer: c

2. Interpolation provides a mean for estimating functions
a) At the beginning points
b) At the ending points
c) At the intermediate points
d) None of the mentioned

Answer: c

3. Interpolation methods are
a) Linear interpolation
b) Piecewise constant interpolation
c) Polynomial interpolation
d) All of the mentioned

Answer: d

4. Linear interpolation is
a) Easy
b) Precise
c) Easy & Precise
d) None of the mentioned

Answer: a

5. Error is equal to

a) Distance between the data points
b) Square of the distance between the data points
c) Half the distance between the data points
d) None of the mentioned

Answer: b

6. Which produces smoother interpolants?

a) Polynomial interpolation
b) Spline interpolation
c) Polynomial & Spline interpolation
d) None of the mentioned

Answer: c

7. Which is more expensive?

a) Polynomial interpolation
b) Linear interpolation
c) Polynomial & Linear interpolation
d) None of the mentioned

Answer: a

8. Gaussian process is a _____ interpolation process.

a) Linear
b) Non linear
c) Not an interpolation process
d) None of the mentioned

Answer: a

9. Interpolation means

a) Adding new data points
b) Only aligning old data points
c) Only removing old data points
d) None of the mentioned

Answer: a

10. Interpolation is a method of

a) Interrelating
b) Estimating
c) Integrating
d) Combining

Answer: b

SAQ

1. What is meant by interpolation? Comment on the necessity and usefulness of interpolation.

2. Define finite differences. Show that i second differences of a quadratic function are constants and the third differences of a cubic function are constants.

3. State and derive Newton's Forward and Backward interpolation formulae. Discuss the difference between the two.

4. Explain what you mean by 'interpolation'. Define the operators A and E in this connection and establish the relation between the two. State the various uses of the two operators and E in connection with the problem of interpolation.

5. Derive Lagrange's interpolation formula and state its uses.

6. If $u_1 = (12 - x)(4 + x)$, $_2 = (5x)(4x)$, $z = (x + 18)(x + 6)$ and $u = 94$, obtain a value of x such that second differences are constants.

7. What is meant by inverse interpolation

8. Write down lagrange's inverse interpolation formula.

9. Find the polynomial function f (x) for which it is known that

(i) $f(0) = 1$, $f(1) = 10$, $f(2)=49$ and $f(3) = 142$

(ii) $f(0) + f(1) + f(2)=5$, $f(3) + f(4) = 20$ and $f(5) = 21$.

10. Write down Newton's forward formula.

CHAPTER TWELVE

SET THEORY

MCQ

Question 1.

If A, B and C are any three sets, then $A - (B \cup C)$ is equal to

(a) $(A - B) \cup (A - C)$

(b) $(A - B) \cup C$

(c) $(A - B) \cap C$

(d) $(A - B) \cap (A - C)$

Answer d

Question 2.

$(A')' = ?$

(a) $U - A$

(b) A'

(c) U

(d) A

Answer-d

Question 3.

$A - B$ is read as?

(a) Difference of A and B of B and A

(b) None of the above

(c) Difference of B and A

(d) Both a and b

Answer-a

Question 4.

If A, B and C are any three sets, then $A \times (B \cup C)$ is equal to

(a) $(A \times B) \cup (A \times C)$

(b) (A ∪ B) × (A ∪ C)

(c) None of these

(d) (A × B) ∩ (A × C)

Answer-a

Question 5.

IF A = [5, 6, 7] and B = [7, 8, 9] then A ∪ B is equal to

(a) [5, 6, 7, 8, 9]

(b) [5, 6, 7]

(c) [7, 8, 9]

(d) None of these

Answer-a

Question 6.

Which of the following sets are null sets

(a) {x: |x |< -4, x ?N}

(b) 2 and 3

(c) Set of all prime numbers between 15 and 19

(d) {x: x < 5, x > 6}

Answer-b

Question 7.

IF R = {(2, 1),(4, 3),(4, 5)}, then range of the function is?

(a) Range R = {2, 4}

(b) Range R = {1, 3, 5}

(c) Range R = {2, 3, 4, 5}

(d) Range R {1, 1, 4, 5}

Answer-b

Question 8.

The members of the set S = {x | x is the square of an integer and x < 100} is

(a) {0, 2, 4, 5, 9, 58, 49, 56, 99, 12}

(b) {0, 1, 4, 9, 16, 25, 36, 49, 64, 81}

(c) {1, 4, 9, 16, 25, 36, 64, 81, 85, 99}

(d) {0, 1, 4, 9, 16, 25, 36, 49, 64, 121}

Answer-b

Question 9.

In a class of 120 students numbered 1 to 120, all even numbered students opt for Physics, whose numbers are divisible by 5 opt for Chemistry and those whose numbers are divisible by 7 opt for Math. How many opt for none of the three subjects?

(a) 19
(b) 41
(c) 21
(d) 57

Answer-b

Question 10.

{ (A, B) : $A^2 + B^2 = 1$} on the sets has the following relation

(a) reflexive
(b) symmetric
(c) none
(d) reflexive and transitive

Answer-b

Question 11.

Two finite sets have N and M elements. The number of elements in the power set of first set is 48 more than the total number of elements in power set of the second test. Then the value of M and N are

(a) 7, 6
(b) 6, 4
(c) 7, 4
(d) 6, 3

Answer-b

Question 12.

The range of the function $f(x) = 3x - 2$, is

(a) $(-\infty, \infty)$
(b) $R - \{3\}$
(c) $(-\infty, 0)$
(d) $(0, -\infty)$

Answer-a

Question 13.

If A, B, C be three sets such that $A \cup B = A \cup C$ and $A \cap B = A \cap C$, then,

(a) B = C
(b) A = C
(c) A = B = C
(d) A = B

Answer-a

Question 14.

In 2nd quadrant?

(a) $X < 0, Y < 0$

(b) $X < 0, Y > 0$
(c) $X > 0, Y > 0$
(d) $X > 0, Y < 0$

Answer-b

Question 15.

How many rational and irrational numbers are possible between 0 and 1?

(a) 0
(b) Finite
(c) Infinite
(d) 1

Answer-c

Question 16.

Empty set is a?

(a) Finite Set
(b) Invalid Set
(c) None of the above
(d) Infinite Set

Answer-a

Question 17.

If A = [5, 6, 7] and B = [7, 8, 9] then A U B is equal to

(a) [5, 6, 7, 8, 9]
(b) [5, 6, 7]
(c) [7, 8, 9]
(d) None of these

Answer-a

Question 18.

Which of the following two sets are equal?

(a) A = {1, 2} and B = {1}
(b) A = {1, 2} and B = {1, 2, 3}
(c) A = {1, 2, 3} and B = {2, 1, 3}
(d) A = {1, 2, 4} and B = {1, 2, 3}

Answer-c

Question 19.

In a class of 50 students, 10 did not opt for math, 15 did not opt for science and 2 did not opt for either. How many students of the class opted for both math and science.

(a) 24
(b) 25

(c) 26
(d) 27
Answer-d
Question 20.
In last quadrant?
(a) X < 0, Y > 0
(b) X < 0, Y < 0
(c) X > 0, Y < 0
(d) X > 0, Y > 0
Answer-d

SAQ

1. Write the solution set of the equation x2 – 4=0 in roster form.
2. Write the set A = {1, 4, 9, 16, 25, . . . } in set-builder form
3. Write an example of a finite and infinite set in set builder form
4. Write an example of equal sets.
5. Write the subsets of {1,2,3}.
6. Write {x: x ∈ R, 3 ≤ x ≤ 4} as intervals.
7. Write the interval (6, 12) in set builder form.
8. If set A = {1, 3, 5}, B = {2, 4, 6} and C = {0, 2, 4, 6, 8}. Then write the universal set for all three sets.
9. If A = { 2, 4, 6, 8} and B = { 6, 8, 10, 12}. Find A ∪ B.
10. If A = { 2, 4, 6, 8} and B = { 6, 8, 10, 12}. Find A ∩ B.
11. If A = {1, 2, 3, 4}, B = {3, 4, 5, 6}, C = {5, 6, 7, 8}. Find A ∪ B ∪ C.
12. If A = {3, 5, 7, 9, 11}, B = {7, 9, 11, 13}, C = {11, 13, 15}. Find A ∩ (B ∪ C).
13. If A = { 1, 2, 3, 4, 5, 6}, B – { 2, 4, 6, 8 }. Find A – B and B – A.
14. If U = {1, 2, 3, 4, 5, 6, 7, 8, 9, 10} and A = {1, 3, 5, 7, 9}. Find A′.
15. Check whether the given sets are equal sets: A = {1, 2, 3, 4} and B = {2, 4, 1, 3}.
16. Write the subsets for the set A = {1, 3, 5, 7}
17. Write the set A = {1, 2, 3, 4, 5, ...} in set-builder form.
18. If A = {1, 3, 5, 7, 9, 11} and B = {1, 2, 3, 13}, the find A-B and B-A.
19. Find A∪(B∪C), if A = {1, 3, 5}, B = {2, 4, 6} and C = {1, 5, 7}.
20. If two sets A and B are having 99 elements in common, then the number of elements common to each of the sets A x B and B x A are?

21. Of the members of three athletic teams in a school 21 are in the cricket team, 26 are in the hockey team and 29 are in the football team. Among them, 14 play hockey and cricket, 15 play hockey and football, and 12 play football and cricket. Eight play all the three games. The total number of members in the three athletic teams is?

22. If a set A has n elements, then the total number of subsets of A is?

23. If (1, 3), (2, 5) and (3, 3) are three elements of A x B and the total number of elements in A x B is 6, then the remaining elements of A x B are?

24. A class has 175 students. The following data shows the number of students obtaining one or more subjects. Mathematics 100, Physics 70, Chemistry 40; Mathematics and Physics 30, Mathematics and Chemistry 28, Physics and Chemistry 23; Mathematics, Physics and Chemistry 18. How many students have offered Mathematics alone?

25. In a town of 10,000 families it was found that 40% family buy newspaper A, 20% buy newspaper B and 10% families buy newspaper C, 5% families buy A and B, 3% buy B and C and 4% buy A and C. If 2% families buy all the three newspapers, then number of families which buy A only is?

26. In a city 20 percent of the population travels by car, 50 percent travels by bus and 10 percent travels by both car and bus. Then persons travelling by car or bus is?

27. A set contains 2n + 1 elements. The number of subsets of this set containing more than n elements is equal to?

28. 20 teachers of a school either teach mathematics or physics. 12 of them teach mathematics while 4 teach both the subjects. Then the number of teachers teaching physics only is?

29. In a battle 70% of the combatants lost one eye, 80% an ear, 75% an arm, 85% a leg, x% lost all the four limbs. The minimum value of x is?

30. If n(A) = 4, n(B) = 3, n(A x B x C) = 24, then n(C) =?

CHAPTER THIRTEEN

PROBABILITY THEORY

MCQ

1. When we throw a coin then what is the probability of getting head?

A. 1/2

B. 3

C. 4

D. 1

Answer - A

2. When we throw a coin then what is the probability of getting a tail?

A. 2

B. 1/2

C. 5

D. 0

Answer - B

3. When we tossed three unbiased coins then what is the probability of getting at least 2 tails?

A. 1/6

B. 1/3

C. 1/2

D. 0

Answer - C

4. When we throw a dice then what is the probability of getting the number greater than 5?

A. 1/5

B. 1/6

C. 1/2

D. 1/3

Answer - B

5. When we throw two dice then what is the probability of getting a sum 9?

A. 2/9

B. 1/12

C. 1/9

D. All of these

Answer - C

6. Events which can never occur together In probability theories then it is classified as?

A. mutually exclusive events

B. collectively exclusive events

C. mutually exhaustive events

D. None of these

Answer - A

7. If J and K will be two variables then the Joint probability of independent events J and K is equal to?

A. P(J) + P(K)

B. P(J) * P(K)

C. P(J) * P(K) – P(J * K)

D. P(J) * P(K) + P(J-K)

Answer - B

8. All possible outcomes for a random experiment are called?

A. sample space

B. event space

C. numerical space

D. both b and c

Answer - D

9. What is the marginal probability of dependent events and independent events?

A. one

B. different

C. same

D. All of these

Answer - C

10. When we consider an event B then non-occurrence of event B is?

A. A is equal to zero

B. intersection of A

C. complement of A
D. union of A
Answer - C

SAQ

(1) A part-time student is taking two courses namely, Statistics and Finance. The probability that the student will pass the statistics course is 0.60 and the probability of passing the finance course is 0.70. Find the probability that the student (i) will pass at least one course (ii) will fail both courses

(2) A machine contains a component C that is vital to its operation. The reliability of component C is 80%. To improve the reliability of a machine, a similar component is used in parallel to form a system. The machine will work provided that one of these components functions correctly. Calculate the reliability of the system S.

(3) India plays two matches each with West Indies and Australia. In any match the probability of India getting points 0, 1 and 2 are 0.45, 0.05 and 0.50 respectively. Assuming that the outcomes are independent, find the probability of India getting at least 7 points.

(4) A class consists of 80 students, 25 of them girls and 55 boys. While 10 of them are rich and the remaining poor, it is found that 20 are fair complexioned. What is the probability of selecting a fair complexioned rich girl or a poor boy who is not fair complexioned?

(5) Suppose the probability for A to win a game against B is 0.4. If A has an option of playing either a "best of 3 games" or a "best of 5 games" match against B, which option should A choose so that the probability of his winning the match is higher? (No game ends in a draw).

(6) A speak the truth in 70% cases and B speaks the truth in 80% cases. What is the probability that they will say the same thing while describing a single event?

(7) The chances that doctor A will diagnose a disease X is 60%. The chances that a patient will die by his treatment after correct diagnosis is 40% and the chances of death by wrong diagnosis is 70%. A patient of doctor A who had disease X, died. What is the chance that his disease was diagnosed correctly?

(8) An anti-aircraft gun can take a maximum of four shots on enemy's plane moving away from it. The probabilities of hitting the plane at first,

second, third and fourth shots are 0.4, 0.3, 0.2 and 0.1 respectively. Find the probability that the gun hits the plane.

(9) A lot contains 20 articles. The probability that the lot contains exactly 2 defective articles is 0.4 and that it contains exactly 3 defective articles is 0.6. Articles are drawn from the lot at random one by one without replacement and tested till all the defective articles are found. What is the probability that this procedure ends at the twelfth testing?

(10) A box contains 2 black, 4 white and 3 red balls. One ball is drawn at a time randomly from the box till all the balls are drawn from it. Find the probability that the balls drawn are in the sequence of 2 black, 4 white and 3 red.

(11) An urn contains 5 balls. Two balls are drawn and found to be white. What is the probability that all the balls are white?

(12) An urn contains 10 white and 15 red balls. Two balls are drawn at random in succession. Find the probabilities of two balls together by virtue of the sampling (i) with replacement, and (ii) without replacement

(13) In a bolt factory, machines A, B and C manufacture 25%, 35% and 40% of the total output respectively. Of their outputs, 5%, 4% and 2% are defective bolts. A bolt is chosen at random and found to be defective. What will be the probability that the bolt came from machine A, B and C?

(14) A factory manufacturing televisions has four units A, B, C and D. The units A, B, C, D manufacture 15%, 20%, 30% and 35% of the total output respectively. It was found that out of their output 1%, 2%, 2% and 3% are defective. A television is chosen at random from the total output, and found Probability to be defective. What is the probability that it came from unit D?

(15) If 20% of the bolts produced by a machine are defective, determine the probability that out of 4 bolts chosen at random (i) 1 (ii) 0 (iii) At most 2 bolts will be defective.

(16) Numbers are selected at random, one at a time, from the two-digit numbers 00, 01, 02, . . . , 99 with replacement. An event E occurs if and only if the product of the two digits of a selected number is 18. If four number is selected, find the probability that the event E occurs at least 3 times.

(17) (i) If a new drug is found to be effective 40% of the time, then what is the probability that in a random sample of 4 patients, it will be effective on 2 of them? (ii) In a manufacturing process, a packaging machine produces 5% defective packages. Find the mean and the standard deviation of the number of defective packages in a random sample of 60 packages.

(18) A multiple choice test contains 6 questions. Each question has 3 answers of which only 1 is the correct answer. The student has no idea as to which of the alternatives is the correct one. The student rolls a fair dice. If face 1 or 2 show up, he selects answer (a). If face 3 or 4 show up, he selects answer (b) and if face 5 or 6 show up, he selects answer (c). Find the probability that he will get (i) exactly 4 correct answers, (ii) no correct answer (iii) at most 2 correct answers.

(19) Assume that the probability of an individual coal miner being killed in a mine accident during a year is 1/2400. Use appropriate distribution to calculate the probability that in mine employing 200 miners, there will be at least one such accident in a year.

(20) In a certain factory producing cycle tyres there is a small chance of 1 in 500 tyres to be defective. The tyres are supplied in lots of 10. Using Poisson distribution, calculate the approximate number of lots containing no defective, one defective, and two defective tyres, respectively, in a consignment of 10,000 lots.

(21) Students of a class were given an aptitude test. Their marks were found to be normally distributed with mean 60 and standard deviation 5. What percentage of students scored more than 60 marks?

(22) The heights of soldiers are normally distributed. If 11.51% of the soldiers are taller than 70.4 inches and 9.68% are shorter than 65.4 inches, find the mean and the standard deviation for the data of heights of soldiers.

CHAPTER FOURTEEN

DISTRIBUTION THEORY

MCQ

1. In a Binomial Distribution, if 'n' is the number of trials and 'p' is the probability of success, then the mean value is given by ___________

a) np

b) n

c) p

d) np(1-p)

Answer: a

2. In a Binomial Distribution, if p, q and n are probability of success, failure and number of trials respectively then variance is given by ___________

a) np

b) npq

c) np2q

d) npq2

Answer: b

3. In a Binomial Distribution, the mean and variance are equal.

a) True

b) False

Answer: b

4. It is suitable to use Binomial Distribution only for ___________

a) Large values of 'n'

b) Fractional values of 'n'

c) Small values of 'n'

d) Any value of 'n'

Answer: c

5. For larger values of 'n', Binomial Distribution ____________

a) loses its discreteness

b) tends to Poisson Distribution

c) stays as it is

d) gives oscillatory values

Answer: b

6. Binomial Distribution is a ____________

a) Continuous distribution

b) Discrete distribution

c) Irregular distribution

d) Not a Probability distribution

Answer B

7. In a Poisson Distribution, if 'n' is the number of trials and 'p' is the probability of success, then the mean value is given by?

a) m = np

b) m = (np)2

c) m = np(1-p)

d) m = p

Answer: a

8. If 'm' is the mean of a Poisson Distribution, then variance is given by ____________

a) m2

b) m1⁄2

c) m

d) m⁄2

Answer: c

9. If 'm' is the mean of a Poisson Distribution, the standard deviation is given by ____________

a) (m)^0.5

b) m2

c) m

d) m⁄2

Answer: a

10. In a Poisson Distribution, the mean and variance are equal.

a) True

b) False

Answer: a

11. Poisson distribution is applied for ____________

a) Continuous Random Variable

b) Discrete Random Variable

c) Irregular Random Variable

d) Uncertain Random Variable

Answer: B

12. In a Poisson distribution, the mean and standard deviation are equal.

a) True

b) False

Answer: b

13. The recurrence relation between P(x) and P(x +1) in a Poisson distribution is given by ____________

a) $P(x+1) - m\,P(x) = 0$

b) $m\,P(x+1) - P(x) = 0$

c) $(x+1)\,P(x+1) - m\,P(x) = 0$

d) $(x+1)\,P(x) - x\,P(x+1) = 0$

Answer: c

14. Normal Distribution is applied for ____________

a) Continuous Random Distribution

b) Discrete Random Variable

c) Irregular Random Variable

d) Uncertain Random Variable

Answer: a

15. The shape of the Normal Curve is ____________

a) Bell Shaped

b) Flat

c) Circular

d) Spiked

Answer: a

16. Normal Distribution is symmetric is about ____________

a) Variance

b) Mean

c) Standard deviation

d) Covariance

Answer: b

17. For a standard normal variate, the value of mean is?

a) ∞

b) 1
c) 0
d) not defined
Answer: c

18. The area under a standard normal curve is?

a) 0
b) 1
c) ∞
d) not defined
Answer: b

19. The standard normal curve is symmetric about the value __________

a) 0.5
b) 1
c) ∞
d) 0
Answer: d

20. Normal Distribution is also known as __________

a) Cauchy's Distribution
b) Laplacian Distribution
c) Gaussian Distribution
d) Lagrangian Distribution
Answer: c

21. Skewness of Normal distribution is __________

a) Negative
b) Positive
c) 0
d) Undefined
Answer: c

22. In Normal distribution, the highest value of ordinate occurs at __________

a) Mcan
b) Variance
c) Extremes
d) Same value occurs at all points
Answer: a

23. The shape of the normal curve depends on its __________

a) Mean deviation

b) Standard deviation
c) Quartile deviation
d) Correlation

Answer: b

24. The value of constant 'e' appearing in normal distribution is ____________

a) 2.5185
b) 2.7836
c) 2.1783
d) 2.7183

Answer: d

25. In Standard normal distribution, the value of mode is ____________

a) 2
b) 1
c) 0
d) Not fixed

Answer: c

SAQ

1. What is meant by Theoretical Distribution/Probability Distribution?
2. What is the difference between theoretical distributions and observed frequency distributions?
3. How are theoretical distributions useful?
4. Define binomial distribution. Give four examples of binomial distribution.
5. Under what conditions can a binomial distribution be applied?
6. State the important characteristics of binomial distribution.
7. State the important properties of binomial distribution.
8. Prove that mean of the binomial distribution is np.
9. Prove that variance of the binomial distribution is npq.
10. For a binomial distribution, mean = 4 and variance = 6. Comment.
11. Define Poisson distribution. Give four examples of Poisson distribution.
12. Under what conditions can a Poisson distribution be applied?
13. State the important characteristics of Poisson distribution.

14. When can the Poisson distribution be used to approximate the binomial distribution?

15. Under what conditions does the binomial distribution tend to be normal distribution?

16. For a Poisson distribution, Mean = 8 and Variance = 7. Comment.

17. Discuss briefly the importance of normal distribution for statistical inference.

18. How is the probability distribution of a discrete random variable defined? Define its expected value.

19. Distinguish between binomial and normal distribution.

20. Distinguish between poisson & normal distribution.

21. Define normal distribution. Give four examples of normal distribution. Describe with a graphical sketch

22. Under what conditions can a normal distribution be applied?

23. State the important characteristics of normal distribution.

24. Can a normal probability distribution be fully determined if we know its mean and standard deviation?

25. Under what conditions does the binomial distribution tend to be a normal distribution?

26, Under what conditions does the Poisson distribution tend to be a normal distribution?

27. Describe the nature of normal curve and its applications.

28. Represent density function in terms of standard normal variable.

29. Represent probability function or density function.

30. How do you fit a normal curve?

CHAPTER FIFTEEN

STATISTICAL INFERENCE THEORY

MCQ

1. Of the following sampling methods, which is a probability method?

a) Judgement

b) Quota

c) Simple random

d) Convenience

Answer: c

2.Which among the following is the benefit of using simple random sampling?

a) The results are always representative.

b) Interviewers can choose respondents freely.

c) Informants can refuse to participate.

d) We can calculate the accuracy of the results.

Answer: d

3. Increasing the sample size has the following effect upon the sampling error?

a) It increases the sampling error

b) It reduces the sampling error

c) It has no effect on the sampling error

d) All of the above

Answer: b

4. Which of the following is not a type of non-probability sampling?

a) Quota sampling

b) Convenience sampling

c) Snowball sampling

d) Stratified random sampling

Answer: d

5. Sample is regarded as a subset of?

(a) Data

(b) Set

(c) Distribution

(d) Population

Answer: d

6. The difference between a statistic and the parameter is called:

(a) Non-random

(b) Probability

(c) Sampling error

(d) Random

Answer: c

7. The probability of selecting an item in probability sampling, from the population is known and is:

(a) Equal to one

(b) Equal to zero

(c) Non zero

(d) None of the above

Answer: c

8. The distribution that is formed by all possible values of a statistics is known as:

(a) Hypergeometric distribution

(b) Normal distribution

(c) Sampling distribution

(d) Binomial distribution

Answer: c

9. Among these, which sampling is based on equal probability?

(a) Simple random sampling

(b) Stratified random sampling

(c) Systematic sampling

(d) Probability sampling

Answer: a

10. The difference between the expected value of a statistic and the value of the parameter being estimated is called a:

(a) Standard error

(b) Bias
(c) Sampling error
(d) Non-sampling error
Answer: b

11. A statement made about a population for testing purpose is called?
a) Statistic
b) Hypothesis
c) Level of Significance
d) Test-Statistic
Answer: b

12. If the assumed hypothesis is tested for rejection considering it to be true is called?
a) Null Hypothesis
b) Statistical Hypothesis
c) Simple Hypothesis
d) Composite Hypothesis
Answer: a

13. A statement whose validity is tested on the basis of a sample is called?
a) Null Hypothesis
b) Statistical Hypothesis
c) Simple Hypothesis
d) Composite Hypothesis
Answer: b

14. A hypothesis which defines the population distribution is called?
a) Null Hypothesis
b) Statistical Hypothesis
c) Simple Hypothesis
d) Composite Hypothesis
Answer: c

15. If the null hypothesis is false then which of the following is accepted?
a) Null Hypothesis
b) Positive Hypothesis
c) Negative Hypothesis
d) Alternative Hypothesis.
Answer: d

16. The rejection probability of Null Hypothesis when it is true is called as?

a) Level of Confidence

b) Level of Significance

c) Level of Margin

d) Level of Rejection

Answer: b

17. The point where the Null Hypothesis gets rejected is called as?

a) Significant Value

b) Rejection Value

c) Acceptance Value

d) Critical Value

Answer: d

18. If the Critical region is evenly distributed then the test is referred as?

a) Two tailed

b) One tailed

c) Three tailed

d) Zero tailed

Answer: a

19. The type of test is defined by which of the following?

a) Null Hypothesis

b) Simple Hypothesis

c) Alternative Hypothesis

d) Composite Hypothesis

Answer: c

20. Which of the following is defined as the rule or formula to test a Null Hypothesis?

a) Test statistic

b) Population statistic

c) Variance statistic

d) Null statistic

Answer: a

21. The process of drawing inferences about the population parameter.

A. Statistical Inference

B. Statistical Analysis

C. both b and c

D. None of these

Answer- A

22. No. of branches of statistical inference are.

A. Three

B. Two

C. Four

D. Five

Answer-B

23. Estimation is the branch of.

A. Statistic

B. Statistical Method

C. Both A andB

D. Statistical Inference

Answer-D

24. Testing of hypothesis is the branch of.

A. Statistical Method

B. Statistical Inference

C. Both A andB

D. None of these

Answer-A

25. The process of finding true but unknown value of populationparameter is called.

A. Statistical Inference

B. Estimation

C. Both B and C

D. None of these

Answer-B

26. Part of population is called.

A. Statistical Inference

B. Statistical Analysis

C. Sample

D. None of these

Answer-C

27. Types of estimation are.

A. Two

B. Three

C. One

D. Four

Answer-A

28. The formula uses to estimate the true but unknown value of population parameter is called an.

A. Estimation

B. Estimate

C. Estimator

D. None of these

Answer-C

29. The value which is obtain by applying an estimator on sample information is known as an.

A. Estimation

B. Estimator

C. Both A&B

D. Estimate

Answer-D

30. Statistic may be an.

A. Estimator

B. Estimate

C. Both A & B

D. None of these

Answer-C

31. The properties of an estimator are.

A. Unbiasedness

B. Sufficiency

C. Consistency

D. All of these

Answer-D

32. Different method of estimation are deals with.

A. Point estimation

B. Interval estimation

C. Both A & B

D. None of these

Answer-C

33. If expected value of an estimator is equal to its respective parameter then it is called an.

A. Biased estimator

B. Unbiased estimator

C. Estimator

D. None of these

Answer-B

34. If expected value of an estimator is greater than the parameter then estimator is called.

A. Unbiasedness

B. Positively Biased

C. Efficiency

D. None of these

Answer-B

35. If expected value of an estimator is equal to its respective parameter then this property known is.

A. Biasedness

B. Estimation

C. Unbiasedness

D. Both B & C

Answer-C

SAQ

1. State the meaning and objects of sampling.
2. What is meant by sample, sample size and statistical laws?
3. State the meaning, properties and usefulness of sampling distribution.
4. State the meaning and usefulness of standard error. Also state why does standard error arise?
5. Define statistical inference. State the two uses problems in statistical inference.
6. Explain the methods of estimating a population parameter.
7. What is a point estimation? Explain the criteria for a good estimation.
8. Explain the terms unbiasedness, consistency, efficiency and sufficiency of an estimate.
9. What is interval estimation? State the meaning and significance of confidence limits.

10. How are the approximate confidence limits and almost sure limits for large samples calculated?

11. **Distinguish between the following:**

(a) Parameter and Statistic

(b) Large Small and Small Sample

(c) Point Estimation and Interval Estimation

12. **Explain the following terms:**

(a) Unbiased Estimates

(b) Efficient Estimate

(c) Point Estimate

(d) Interval Estimate

(e) Confidence Limits

13. **State whether you would prefer a large sample or a small sample in the following cases:**

(a) The degree of availability of the data is not much.

(b) A higher degree of confidence is desired.

(c) In case of test-check where internal control is found to be ineffective.

(d) Previous experience reveals a low rate of error.

14. **Explain the following terms:**

(a) Statistical Significance

(b) Test Statistic

(c) Critical Region

(d) Power of Test

(e) Degrees of Freedom

(f) Assumptions relating to large Samples theory,

15. (a) Why is the knowledge of sampling distribution important in statistical theory? (b) Why should there be different formulac for testing the significance of the difference between measure when the samples are (i) small (ii) large?

16. List the practical steps involved in testing hypothesis.

17. **Distinguish between the following:**

(a) Null hypothesis and Alternative Hypothesis.

(b) Two-tailed Tests and One-tailed tests.

(c) Right tailed test and Left tailed tests.

(d) Type I Error and Type II Error.

18. **In the following cases, state which test out of Z-test, t-test, x^2 -test, f-test, is appropriate?**

(a) To test the significance for attributes,

(b) To test the significance of the mean of a sample of 50

(c) To test the significance of the mean of a sample of 29 where a is known

(d) To test the significance of the means of a sample of 29 where o is not known.

(e) To test the significance of the difference between the means of two samples of size 50 each if (i) o, and a, are known (ii) if o, and o, are not known.

(f) To test the significance of the difference between the means of two samples of size 29 each where o, and o, are known.

(g) To test the significance of the difference between the means of two samples of size 29 each where o, and o, are not known.

(h) To test the significance of standard deviation of a random sample of 29 when mean is known.

(I) To test the significance of standard deviation of a random sample of 29 when mean is not known.

(J) To test the significance of the difference between the standard deviations of two samples of size 29 each where means (X, & X.) are known.

(k) To test the significance of the difference between the standard deviations of two samples of size 29 each where mean (X, & X,) are not known.

(L) To test for goodness of fit.

(m) To test for independence of attributes.

19. **Name the test of significance which is most appropriate in the following situations:**

(a) For judging the significance of differences of more than two sample means at one and the same time.

(b) For comparing a sample variance to a specified variance of the population.

(c) For comparing the mean of a random sample to some hypothesised mean for the population when n = 15 and population variance is known.

20. What is t-test?

21. State the conditions for the use of t-test.

22. State the properties of t-distribution.

23. State the applications of t-distribution.

24. What is distribution? State its important properties.

25. What is a test? Under what conditions is it applicable?

26. **Write short notes on:**

(a) Yates's correction for continuity

(b) Grouping in case of small theoretical frequencies

(c) Goodness of fit

27. State the important uses of x^2 test.

28. How is test used to test for a specified variance?

29. How is a test used to test the independence of attributes?

30. How is a test used to test the goodness of fit?

31. (a) What is analysis of variance?

(b) Where is it used? Give two examples.

32. Distinguish between one-way and two way classification.

33. State the basic assumptions made for analysis of variance.

34. Briefly describe the procedure followed in one factor analysis of variance.

35. Briefly describe the procedure followed in two factor analysis of variance.

36. What is 'Statistical Decision Theory'?

37. Enumerate the components of a problem.

38. Enumerate the types of problems in decision making under different environment.

39. **Write short notes on the following:**

(a) Statistical Decision Theory

(b) Deterministic Problems

(c) Stochastic Problems

(d) Problems under Uncertainty

(e) Maximax Decision Criterion

(f) Maxmin or Wald Decision Criterion

(g) Minimax Decision Critierion or Regret Criterion

(h) Hurwicz Criterion

(i) Laplace Decision Criterian

40. Write the fullform of EMV & EVPI

Printed by Libri Plureos GmbH in Hamburg,
Germany